MW00963986

*Heart to Heart*
S E R I E S

# Helping You Start Again

BOBB AND CHERYL BIEHL

BROADMAN
& HOLMAN
PUBLISHERS

Nashville, Tennessee

# Helping You
# Start Again

Published by:
Broadman & Holman Publishers

Printed in the United States of America

Design: Steven Boyd
4262-74
0-8054-6274-0

Dewey Decimal Classification: 306.81
Subject Heading: MARRIAGE
Library of Congress Card Catalog Number: 95-45309

**Library of Congress Cataloging-in-Publication Data**
Biehl, Bobb.
   Pre-remarriage questions: helping you start again / by Bobb
and Cheryl Biehl
       p.   cm.   (Heart to heart series)
   ISBN 0-8054-6274-0
   1. Remarriage—United States—Miscellanea.  2.
Communication in marriage—United States—Miscellanea.—
I. Biehl, Cheryl.  II. Title.  III. Series.
   HQ1019.U6B54   1996
   306.84—dc20

   95-45309
   CIP

00 99  98  97  96  5  4  3  2  1

# Contents

✧

Introduction

# A Note from the Authors

If you ask enough of the right questions before you remarry, your new marriage will start on a much more solid foundation. Having candid, open, frank discussions before you say "I do" also substantially reduces the number of marriage-jarring "explosions" which can happen in the first year of any marriage.

We believe that the agonizing, heart-wrenching process of divorce many times *can* be prevented by asking the right questions and processing the answers *before* remarriage.

We believe that you want your marriage to go beyond just "staying together till the kids leave home," and that you want a rich intimacy not possible in any other relationship.

We have created more than 200 questions that can strengthen your relationship. These questions cover most of the major problem areas you are likely to face as a couple. The more you know about how your fiancé thinks and feels about these issues and the more discussions you have *before* you remarry, the better decision you will make.

If this book can give you a new perspective in even a few areas in your relationship, we will feel every hour we have invested in creating this book was worth a thousand times the effort.

It is our hope and prayer that you will have wisdom, patience, and understanding as you work your way through these candid, relationship-building questions!

Bobb and Cheryl Biehl

# PART ONE

# Before You Begin

*If the focus of this book could be summed up
in one word, it would be* decision.
*If you are reading this book,
you may have experience with a decision
like this already.*

# Chapter 1

## *The Remarriage Decision*

Whether your prior marriage ended in divorce or in death, there is much you can learn from it. What things do you wish you had known going into your previous marriage? If you knew then what you know now, would you still have gotten married? Would it have been easier to resolve certain issues before they blew up unexpectedly? Looking back, would it have been wiser to discover areas of agreement and disagreement before you said, "I do"?

The best time to decide whether you will live the rest of your life together is *before* you say "I do," not after!

So much miscommunication that takes place between people is because each person is coming from a different perspective. We assume that we know what we believe, think, and feel, and we assume we know what the other person believes, thinks, and feels. Too often, our assumptions are incorrect. These questions are designed to help identify the underlying assumptions in each area of your life. The clearer you can be about each other's assumptions *before* marriage, the fewer number of surprises after marriage.

Couples considering remarriage today seem more reflective about the remarriage decision than couples were fifteen or twenty years ago. That's good, particularly if a couple has the right decision-making tools and solid premarital counseling. This book can be a significant tool for helping you honestly evaluate your relationship.

Any engagement which cannot stand the asking of these questions does not have a high likelihood of withstanding the pressure of married living in today's society.

It is hard but far easier to break a dating relationship than an engagement.

It is hard but far easier to break an engagement than a marriage after the marriage vows have been spoken and children have been conceived, or born.

Chapter 2

*The Red / Yellow / Green System—*
*Finding "Land Mines" before They Explode*

The candid questions in this book help uncover miscommunications which might otherwise become invisible "landmines" which explode unexpectedly and cause major damage to a relationship. These questions provide a "shovel" you can use to dig out the hidden, emotional mines before you step on them.

We do not wish to put unnecessary stress on a relationship, rather, we desire simply to bring to light those areas in which there may be existing disagreement. This then gives you opportunity to fully enjoy your agreements and to fully explore your disagreements, before your final decision and final commitment.

As you discuss the questions in this book, you may find only three or four that are potentially relationship-threatening disagreements. You can begin to work through these potentially explosive areas during the "deeply in love" part of your relationship.

Suppose you put off the critical discussions on these issues until *after* you are married, possibly have children and have increased financial obligations. If some problem arises and one of these major areas of disagreement must be faced under pressure, it creates a situation in which marriage can blow apart and end in divorce. The devastation of divorce is what these questions are designed to prevent.

## Red / Yellow / Green

A great tool for determining your understanding of each other is the "red/yellow/green light" technique. After you have thoroughly discussed a question, simply mark the question with a pencil in the margin using an *R* (red, for total disagreement), *Y* (yellow, for different conclusions or misunderstanding), or *G* (green, for total agreement).

Your goal is to get to the point where you have many greens in each area, a few yellows, and very few reds. Once a question is green, you might even want to use a bright green marking pen or pencil to highlight those questions so that you can see at a glance just how much you already agree. It's satisfying and reassuring!

Some of the questions do not require that you agree on an "answer"; you are just sharing personal experiences with each other. In that case, just mark it green when you have finished your discussion.

Go back to the yellow questions and discuss them until they turn red or green. Of the questions you mark red, there may be only two or three that actually represent "divorce potential" kinds of conflict. See chapter 11, "How to Turn a Red Light to Green," for help on working through these questions.

## Talk It Out / Write It Out

One of the advantages of these questions is that you can simply talk them out. Depending on your personal preferences, you may even want to tape record some of your discussions to listen to yourselves in twenty years. This will provide great memories for you, and it may be valuable for your sons and daughters to hear the thoughts and feelings of your early married life.

If you are separated for a period of time because of career or school, you may want to write out your answers to preselected questions and send them to each other. In fact, this is a fun way to answer these questions even if you're not apart. Although it might sound like a lot of work at first, writing out your thoughts and feelings actually has many advantages:

✧ Writing gives you time to reflect on the question and think more about how you will answer.

✧ You have a chance to present your answer in totality, without the risk of being interrupted.

✧ Some people find it easier to write something very personal than actually say it out loud.

## Top Ten Simple Ways to Predict a Problem Marriage

1. Getting married to spite someone else

2. Getting married without listening to close friends who are warning you of obvious problems

3. Getting married to someone of a different faith

4. Getting married with concerns and questions you are afraid to ask your fiancé

5. Getting married with things you are hiding from your fiancé that you plan to disclose once the "knot has been tied"

6. Getting married on the rebound—within months of a painful breakup

7. Getting married because you just want to get out of your parents' house

8. Getting married without dating at least twelve months.

9. Getting married based primarily on a relationship of correspondence

10. Getting married because of a fear of never having another chance

These ten ways are not guaranteed to end in divorce. Some marriages make it in spite of built-in problems. But, these are common situations which create major problems and pressures on a marriage and often end in divorce.

If you are in one of the top ten predictable problem marriage situations, it is doubly important that you take this book seriously.

# Chapter 3

*Getting Started*

There are different ways you can approach the questions. Here are a few ideas:

✧ Start with the first category (financial) and proceed down the questions one by one until you have answered them all. Then go to the next category and do the same. Don't forget to mark each question red, yellow, or green.

✧ Decide together on one of the seven areas of life that particularly interests you at the moment. Start with the first question and work your way down, marking each one red, yellow, or green. There is plenty of space so you can make notes in the book about your thoughts.

✧ Answer three questions (or however many you decide) in one category. When those questions have been marked red, yellow, or green, then go to the next chapter and do three questions from that category. After you have answered three from each category, go back and answer three more from each category, and so on.

However you do it, we strongly suggest in each category that you follow the questions in order. You will be surprised at the time you can waste reading all the questions every time you pick up the book. If you simply follow the questions in order, you eliminate the hassle of trying to find the "perfect" question.

If you come to a question that does not apply to your relationship, just skip it and move on. Or, if a question seems too sensitive to discuss, mark it red and come back to it later.

As you answer each of the questions, you will undoubtedly think of additional questions. Write them down in the margin before you forget them. If you're not sure what the question means, just interpret it the way *you* want to.

✦

# PART TWO

# Pre-remarriage Questions

*The questions in this book are divided among seven basic areas of life:*

Financial
Marriage and Family
Personal Growth
Physical
Professional
Social
Spiritual

These seven categories have been listed alphabetically, but this is not to imply that the first on the list (financial) is more important than the last (spiritual). Note that God is not reserved only for the spiritual category. God is the God of families, commerce, hearts, minds, bodies, businesses, and societies, as well as the Lord of His church. So be encouraged to bring up the spiritual element in the discussion of any of the other categories.

✧

# Chapter 4

## *Financial*

There are few areas of married life which cause more yelling, pouting, and throwing of things than the financial area. One of the most frequent reasons given for divorce today is financial struggles and disagreements. To the extent that a couple is making different financial assumptions, it is likely that they will go through their marriage with some severe strains in this area. Discussing your financial assumptions will help reduce the amount of tension in this area.

The financial pressures of remarriage are frequently greater than a first marriage because of alimony, child support, and a wide variety of second marriage complications. Caution: These questions need to be addressed somewhat delicately but, at the same time, openly and honestly.

Make doubly sure your assumptions are compatible. in this area today, and you will be half as likely to divorce tomorrow!

1. If we inherited a million dollars, what would you want to do with it?

2. What percent of our income should we give to the church we attend? Why? What percent of our income should we give to charitable organizations?

3. How much income would you like us to make (together) this next year?

4. How long do you expect both of us to continue working outside the home?

5. Where would you like to live in five years?

6. What do you think about credit cards? How many credit cards do you have now? What are the debts on each? Which cards should we continue to have (if any)?

7. Will our income support the standard of living to which we are accustomed? If not, what adjustments are we willing to make after the wedding?

8. What should we do with my car? Your car? What kind of car would you like to drive in five years? Ten years?

9. About how much should we spend on clothing a year? How much do we currently spend a month?

10. Should we change our checking account arrangements (joint versus separate accounts)?

11. Who should write the checks for our monthly bills? Who should balance the bank statement each month? Why?

12. If we need a larger (or smaller) house, when should we begin planning for it? How can we afford it?

13. Do you think our children should be given a car at age sixteen? Why or why not? If so, how expensive a car, and for what reason?

14. Do you think children should be given an allowance? If so, how much at ages five, ten, fifteen, twenty-one? If not, why not?

15. How much should we spend a year on luxury items such as jewelry, furs, athletic equipment, trips, etc.?

16. What percentage should we tip a server who does an outstanding job? A poor job? An average job?

17. How much should you have to pay to have your hair cut? Styled? What is a suitable tip for these services?

18. How much life insurance should we have? Health insurance? What company? Which agent?

19. How do you feel about borrowing money from our parents, friends, or relatives?

20. How do you feel about loaning money to our parents, friends, or relatives? What if they couldn't pay it back?

21. What percent of our income should we be saving?

22. How would you have the most amount of fun if we only had five dollars to spend some evening?

23. How much should we spend on special occasions like:

   ✧ Birthdays: each other's, parents, children, friends, others

   ✧ Anniversaries: our own, parents, friends, relatives, others

   ✧ Other special days: Mother's Day, Father's Day, Valentine's Day

   ✧ Christmas: each other's gift, parents, children, other relatives, coworkers, friends, Christmas tree, decorations

24. Who should do the gift buying for birthdays? Anniversaries? Christmas? Other special days?

25. How do you feel about declaring bankruptcy? Is it ever OK?

26. What should be the dollar limit on purchases made without the other person's knowledge? Why?

27. What are your feelings about a monthly budget?

28. Prioritize the following household items as to their importance to you.

| | |
|---|---|
| __ Athletic equipment | __ Compact disc player |
| __ Color TV | __ Dining room furniture |
| __ Dishwasher | __ Food dehydrator |
| __ Food processor | __ Freezer |
| __ Hobby items | __ Living room furniture |
| __ Bedroom furniture | __ Microwave |
| __ Piano | __ Stereo system |
| __ VCR | __ Video camera |
| __ Washer/dryer | |
| __ Other: _____ | |

29. What are your total financial obligations right now? Which debts should we try to reduce or eliminate first?

30. What are your financial obligations relating to alimony and child support?

31. What are your feelings about a will? How will each of our families be cared for in our new will?

32. What should the children inherit when we die? If there are children from separate families, how should our assets be distributed?

33. What investments do you have today? How do you see these investments after we are married? Who will

manage them? Are they now a part of our will? Do you want to invest more money? How? When? [Key discussion at this point in the relationship]

34. How would you feel about paying bills that my former spouse created, and I am now obligated to pay?

35. What was the financial settlement from your divorce? May I see your divorce papers?

36. How would you feel about facing financial pressures that may develop in the future relating to my previous marriage? (e.g., How would you feel about appearing in court several more times, costing $5,000 each time?)

37. What are your feelings about a prenuptial agreement? Do we need one to protect ourselves and our assets? [A prenuptial agreement is a written legal statement made *prior* to marriage, stating your intentions regarding each of your assets, debts, etc.]

38. Where should the child support money go? Into a general fund, a separate checking account specifically for the child, etc.?

39. Are you willing to pay for counseling for my children? Children who don't live with us?

## Chapter 5

## *Marriage and Family*

You are not only marrying a single person of the opposite sex, you are determining:

⋄ your future mother-in-law;

⋄ your future father-in-law;

⋄ your children's other parent;

⋄ your future nieces and nephews, and all of the rest of your in-laws;

⋄ one of your grandchildren's other grandparents.

The success or failure of your marriage impacts a lot of people. Communicate honestly and clearly on these issues. There is a lot of family future resting on your discussions.

1. What are some activities that you'd like us to do together?

2. How do you best communicate your feelings about something?

3. When we disagree how should we settle it? How did your parents settle their disagreements?

4. What kind of music do you like the best?

5. What are your three favorite things about loving and being loved?

6. Are there some things in lovemaking that you would like to try? Are there things you do not want to do?

7. From your perspective, what are the five most important things to be aware of when making love?

8. What are the three things you admire most about each of your parents as a marriage partner?

9. What couple, whom you know personally, has the most ideal marriage? Why do you think it is so ideal?

10. What would be the most strictly enforced rules of our house for child discipline?

11. What are your greatest concerns or lingering questions about our married life together? Who could we talk to who would help us understand and deal with our concerns?

12. Are there any habits that I have that you find irritating? Explain.

13. Who will be primarily responsible for the day-to-day cooking, cleaning, and shopping?

14. Do you see divorce as an option for us in any circumstances? If so, in what circumstances?

15. What preventive steps can we take to avoid divorce?

16. What would you do if I became totally incapacitated and I could never have sex or children? What would be your response if I developed cancer or broke my back and was partially paralyzed?

17. What if my job should require me to be away from home a week or two at a time? Do you feel you could

handle being alone that much without being tempted to "run around"? Do you feel I could handle being alone? How would you feel about having the complete responsibility for the house (and children, if any)?

18. What do you think about me going out with my same-gender friends? How often?

19. Do you want to have children? How many?

20. How do you think you would respond if we had a severely disabled child?

21. How do you think you would feel if we were not able to have children? How do you feel about adoption?

22. How do you feel about spanking my child? Under what conditions? How?

23. What do you feel about having our elementary-age children in Sunday School or church? Junior highers? High schoolers?

24. Do you think elementary-age children should be in a public or private school? What about home schooling? What about older children? Why?

25. What five to ten foundational biblical truths do you think should be stressed in the raising of children?

26. At what age should a son begin to date? When should a daughter begin to date? What should be our house rules for curfew?

27. What style of discipline would you use with a toddler? Elementary-age child? Junior higher? High schooler? College-age?

28. How much of a child's college education should be paid by the parents? Under what conditions?

29. How much freedom and responsibility should children be given at age five? Ten? Fifteen?

30. What do you see as your role as a parent with our children? My role?

31. How often should parents get away from babies in their first year, leaving them with baby-sitters? When the kids are older?

32. How do you feel about nursery schools? About day-care centers?

33. How often do you think people should take showers/baths? Brush teeth? Change underwear? Wash out the tub?

34. How do you feel about birth control? If you think we should use something, what method do you think is best for us? How do you feel about surgery?

35. Who do you think is responsible to do the following work around the home?

| | |
|---|---|
| Dishes | House cleaning |
| Yard work | Car repair |
| Dealing with insurance | Getting the Christmas tree |
| Fixing things | Making the bed |
| Washing clothes | Ironing clothes |
| Picking out kids' clothes | Other _____ |

36. How do you feel about an unmade bed in the middle of the day?

37. How often do you feel it is important to go out to dinner rather than cook at home?

38. Describe your idea of an ideal week of evenings?

39. How do you want to celebrate our wedding anniversary each year (in general)?

40. Is there something special you've always wanted to do, but haven't yet had the money or taken the time?

41. How much television do you watch each day? How do you feel about having the television turned on for most of the day?

42. What are your feelings about abortion?

43. What would you do if one of our children wanted to marry someone of another race or ethnic group?

44. If one of your parents became widowed or seriously ill, what should be our responsibility to him/her? If one of *my* parents became widowed or ill?

45. What's involved in "romance" for you? (Be specific.) How important to you are those elements in our marriage?

46. Do you foresee any of our relatives interfering in our marriage? Who? How? What would we do if that happened?

47. How does your mother feel about our relationship? Your father? Brothers and sisters?

48. What are your parent's feelings and attitudes about your divorce? About your former spouse?

49. What are your feelings about living in "his" or "her" house? Would a new "neutral" house be better for us and the children?

50. What kinds of topics are the most difficult for you to talk with me about?

51. What differences do you think there will be in our methods of raising children? How will we resolve these differences and communicate them to the children?

52. How would you feel about paying child support for children who won't be living with you and may not even accept you?

53. What are five reasons, besides love, that you want to marry again?

54. How will you go about developing rapport with my children? How can I best develop rapport with yours?

55. Are there "skeletons" of any kind in your past (bankruptcy, criminal record, abortion, etc.)? [Avoid surprises. Talk these things through before a final commitment, *not* on your honeymoon!]

56. What is your philosophy and theology of marriage? Has that changed at all since your divorce?

57. What are your feelings about seeing my "ex"? About talking with him/her on the phone?

58. What three to five things did you do that may have contributed to the breakup of your marriage? What would you do differently now?

59. Do you think our children should be involved in the decision to remarry? Why? How much?

60. What about child custody? Is it final? What are the existing arrangements? What are your feelings?

61. Would you be willing to adopt my children if the opportunity arose? Why?

62. Assuming I have custody of my children, are you willing to love, raise, and financially support my children (your stepchildren) alone in the event I were to die? How does that make you feel?

63. If we were to get full legal custody of my children in the future, how would that make you feel? Why?

64. How do you feel about the children's "other" grand-parents, for example, having strong influence over our family's holiday and birthday plans?

65. Are you willing to put me first, even before your children?

66. How would you feel about my children being involved in the wedding ceremony? Your children?

67. Do you understand that our honeymoon phase, or "break-in time" to marriage, will be very limited because we have children? How does that make you feel?

68. How might you handle the hostility of my children if they get "bad press" about you from my former spouse's side of the family?

69. What kind of manners do you expect around the house and at mealtime?

70. Because of your past marriage, are there any types of behavior that may frighten your children (loud voices, swearing, ignoring each other, etc.)?

71. What holiday traditions are your children accustomed to?

## Chapter 6

*Personal Growth*

Remember back ten years. Talk about what life was like for each of you then. Could you possibly have imagined where you would be today?

It would have been just as easy for you to imagine today ten years ago as it would be to imagine ten years from now—today!

*Point:* You will both continue to grow rapidly, but how do you each want to grow, and in what direction? Where do you each feel held back?

1. If you could sit and chat with any person in the world, with whom would you talk? What three questions would you ask that person?

2. What do you consider your three greatest strengths? What is your single greatest strength?

3. A year from today, in what three to five areas of your life would you most like to be stronger than you are now?

4. In what area—spiritual, physical, personal growth, marriage and family, social, professional, finan-

cial—would you most like to grow in the next ten years?

5. In what three areas would you most like to see me grow in the next year? Why?

6. What do you feel are the three key things keeping you from reaching your full potential as a person today?

7. If you could become the "world expert" in any one area or subject, what would it be?

8. In what area would you suggest I specialize and become expert?

9. What moral/social/political issues (e.g., abortion, war, rape, drugs, etc.) would you like to know more about? Why?

10. What five books would you most like to read? Why?

11. Name five of your all-time favorite books. What was it about each of these that you liked? Would you like me to read them?

12. What course, seminar, or conference would you most like to attend? Why?

13. If we could improve only one aspect of the way we relate to each other, what would that be? Why?

14. Is there some negative comment someone made about you years ago which is still holding back your confidence? How can I help you overcome that blockage in your life?

15. In what three areas of your life do you think you have grown most in the last several years?

16. What three people have had the greatest impact in your life? How?

17. What single question did you keep asking yourself the most during the past few weeks?

18. If you had four hours in which to do anything you wanted, what would you do? Why? If you had a weekend?

19. How would you describe your self-esteem level right now? Why? What could help strengthen it?

Chapter 7

*Physical*

One basic reality in life is: We all change physically as we grow older.

What are your thoughts about your own physical appearance and that of your fiance?

How do you actually *feel* about your weight, your sex appeal, and your overall image?

1. What five things do you like best about my physical appearance, in general?

2. What first attracted you to me?

3. How do you feel about an exercise program for you and me? What kind? How often?

4. What kind of physical exercise would you most like to do together? Separately?

5. What three suggestions would you like to make about how I can improve my physical appearance?

6. How do you feel about taking vitamins and nutritional supplements? How much per month should we spend on them?

7. Would you prefer to go to a medical doctor or a nutritionist?

8. How do you feel about going to chiropractors?

9. What "turns you off" sexually? What "turns you on" sexually?

10. Based on your family's medical history, do you have any anxieties about your health?

11. How do you feel about me being overweight? How do you feel about you being overweight? How many pounds do you think is overweight?

12. How do you feel about baldness? Wrinkles? Gray hair?

13. Do you have any desire to belong to a recreational club, such as YMCA, or to a country club? Why?

14. Do you have a favorite recreational activity? How often do you participate in it now?

15. How much fresh air do you like when sleeping? If you use an electric blanket, where do you set the temperature—closer to 1 or 10?

16. How do you feel about getting older?

17. What do you plan to do to avoid the potential of having an affair?

18. How do you prefer I wear my hair? How do you feel about beards, mustaches, sideburns? How many buttons should I leave open on a shirt or blouse?

19. How important to you are the following in lovemaking? (Rank: 1=crucial, 2=somewhat important, 3=not necessary for my enjoyment)

| | |
|---|---|
| ___ Personal hygiene | ___ Foreplay |
| ___ The setting | ___ Time available |
| ___ Lack of distractions | ___ Creativity |
| ___ Oils, candles, etc. | ___ Romantic conversation |

___ Garments  ___ Lack of tension
___ Physical energy  ___ Unresolved arguments

20. How do you feel about alcoholic beverages? Cigars or cigarettes? Mind-altering drugs?

21. What are your feelings about pornographic magazines, movies, etc.? Explain.

22. What are your expectations regarding our sexual relationship? What do you think is normal sexual behavior? How often are you expecting to make love?

23. Are you willing to have a physical exam and a blood test? An HIV test? If not, why?

24. If you have had a vasectomy, are you willing to consider a reversal?

25. Have you had any sexual difficulties (physiological or psychological) in your past marriage relationship that could affect our sexual relationship?

26. How do you feel about communicating on sexual issues? Embarrassed? Awkward? Comfortable? Why?

27. To what extent should we display affection for one another in front of the children?

28. Was there infidelity in your last marriage?

29. How could we help our children understand, accept, and control their potential sexual attraction to their stepsisters, stepbrothers, and/or stepparent?

30. What if I am not as "good in bed" as your previous mate?

31. Would you like to know how I feel I compare with your previous mate?

# Chapter 8

## *Professional*

As a person matures he/she moves through phases like "I got the job!" "I think I'll choose this field as my profession." "My career is progressing well . . . or in a slump." "What will my lifework be?"

As each of you progresses in age and professional experience, it is critical that you are both making the same basic assumptions concerning work!

1. What brings you the most satisfaction in your job or career? In the relationships at work?

2. If I decided to go back to school for further education, how would you feel about that decision? Why? What would be the advantages? Disadvantages?

3. How important to you is the feeling that you are making a significant difference in your work?

4. How important is it to you to have fun on your job?

5. How important to you is being a member of the team at work? Of being accepted by that team?

6. How do you feel about my work? What do you like about it? Does anything frustrate or concern you?

7. What would you consider my top three alternative careers? Why do you think these would be good things for me to pursue?

8. To what professional or work-related associations or groups should you or I or we belong? Why?

9. How would you feel about my working with the ———— company?

10. Would you prefer that I be on a lower fixed salary or a higher potential commission with no guaranteed income? Why?

11. What work-related or professional goals will you have to reach to feel successful in life?

12. What will you have to learn, do, or become before you are ready for the next promotion at work?

13. How important is security in any career you would choose? Why?

14. If you could start a business with anyone, what three people would you choose to be partners? Why?

15. What company, organization, or firm would you most like to work with if you had your choice? Why?

16. How do you feel about a job or career for me that would include travel? How much would be acceptable? How much would be unacceptable?

17. How important to you is our parents' acceptance of what I do for employment? Our children's acceptance?

18. If we started a business together, what would you want to do in that business? How would you feel about us working together as a two-person team at some time in the future?

19. If you could have anyone's job in the world, whose job would you have and why?

20. What do you definitely and absolutely *not* want in your lifework?

21. In your heart of hearts, how do you feel about a wife having (not having) a separate career from her husband, where she may need as much support to keep going in her profession as the husband would in his?

22. How would you feel about me making more (or less) money than you do, if that should happen?

23. What is it in a job, profession, or career that you would definitely not want me to be part of in the future?

24. If I had all the time, energy, and money I needed and could have any position or work in the world, what position or work would you ideally like me to have? Why?

25. If my work responsibilities required me to move to another location, in what parts of the world would you feel comfortable living? Where would you definitely not want to live?

26. If my work required a move and yours did not, how would we decide what to do?

27. If I, as the husband, made enough money so that you would not have to work outside the home, would you still want to work, and why?

28. Under what circumstances do you feel a wife should (should not) work outside the home?

29. How would you feel about me working a swing shift? Night shift?

30. How would you feel about me working two jobs?

31. While you were growing up, did your mother work outside the home? Either way, how did you feel about it?

32. If you were ever fired from a job in which you were happy, how would you want me to relate to you when you came home from work?

33. What is the highest position you can imagine me holding at some time in the future?

34. How would you feel about me if I became a: Full-time Christian minister? Corporate executive? Factory worker? Farmer? Lawyer? Medical professional (doctor, nurse, etc.)? Missionary? Movie star? Psychologist? Police officer? Politician? Rock singer? Salesperson? Self-employed? Truck driver?

35. If the career I chose required me to spend three to ten years of preparation before I could become successful, how would you feel about waiting that long?

36. How do you feel about me working with people who knew or know my former spouse?

37. How do you feel about attending work-related seminars and meetings that the spouse is expected to attend?

38. How do you feel about my work, position, status, image? Compared to your former spouse?

# Chapter 9

## *Social*

Friendships are invaluable! Social times are priceless! However, are we making the same assumptions about our social lives? Do we enjoy the same people, going to the same parties, or entertaining in the same way?

1. If you could go to any "high society" event in the world, which would you most enjoy attending? Why?

2. If you could go back in history, what social event would you most enjoy attending? Why?

3. One year from now, what differences (if any) would you anticipate in our social life?

4. How confident are you socially, on a scale of one to ten (where one is insecure and ten is extremely confident)? What are the social situations in which you feel least comfortable and why? What are the social situations in which you feel most confident and why?

5. How do you honestly feel about parties? What kind do you most enjoy? Least? Want to avoid at all costs?

6. What is the best party you've ever attended, and why did you enjoy it?

7. If we were to go with one couple to a foreign country, what country would you want to visit? With whom?

8. Who are your five closest friends and why? Who are five people you used to have as friends but have drifted from? Why did those friendships drift, and how does it make you feel when you reflect on them?

9. When going out for a social evening, what do you enjoy doing most with another couple or small group of people?

10. How do you feel about having friends "pop in"? Your relatives? My relatives?

11. How do you feel about us "popping in" on friends? Your relatives? My relatives?

12. How do you feel about having out-of-town friends stay overnight with us? Out-of-town relatives?

13. How do you feel about staying with friends when we travel, as compared to staying in hotels?

14. If we were to take a trip with another couple within five hundred miles of home, what would you want to do? How long would you want to stay? Where would you want to go? With whom?

15. How many nights a month would you be open to guests staying in our home?

16. What qualities do your friends have in common? What do you look for in a friend?

17. What do you give to a friendship or to a social relationship?

18. Where should we meet new friends (church, work, family, etc.)?

19. How do you feel about your parents' social life? How do you feel about my parents' social life?

20. How many evenings a week (or a month) would you enjoy socializing with friends as a married couple? Why?

21. Who do you consider your top five lifelong friends to be—friends you'd like to remain close to for many years? Why in each case? How do you think I feel about each of your close friends?

22. What do you most enjoy doing on an evening out? Why?

23. If we were given $2,000 to go somewhere just for fun, where would you want to go? Why?

24. If we had $200 to spend socially, how would you want to spend it?

25. If we had only $20 to do something "wild and crazy" together socially, what would you want to do? Why?

26. On a weekend night, if the choice was between staying home and reading or talking, or going out, which would you prefer?

27. If we were to go to dinner on five separate evenings, with five different couples who are married, what five couples would you most enjoy going to dinner with? Why in each case?

28. What are your feelings about attending social events that I also attended with my former spouse?

29. Thinking back to couple friends from our previous marriages, which do we feel comfortable continuing to see? Which will be comfortable with us?

30. What were your most frustrating social times in your previous marriage? Why?

✧

Chapter 10

*Spiritual*

Two American taboos of conversation are politics and religion. In marriage, however, these topics are "must discussions"!

The Bible warns about being "unequally yoked," or being of different faiths as a foundation for your marriage. Take your time and discuss each of these questions as openly as possible. Ten years from now you will be extremely pleased that you did!

1. What are three highlights of your spiritual life?

2. When you lean back in your chair and imagine heaven, what do you see?

3. How do you feel about the church you/we attend? Is the church teaching the truths of the Bible?

4. How often do you want to attend church once we are married?

5. What do you enjoy doing or being involved with in a church?

6. What are the three most important things you have learned from the Bible?

7. How often do you read the Bible? Why?

8. What does prayer mean to you?

9. How do you feel about our having a devotional time together? Why?

10. How would you feel about my being a member of the clergy someday? Why?

11. What was a low point of your spiritual life?

12. What are the important biblical issues, principles, or doctrines? What is nonnegotiable?

13. If you could ask God any three questions on any topic, what would you ask? Why?

14. What do you believe the Bible says about marriage and divorce?

15. How do you feel about and think about Jesus?

16. In what area of your spiritual life do you feel the greatest need for personal growth?

17. From your perspective, what are three keys to a strong spiritual life?

18. If I felt "led of God" to move to Africa and work with some tribal group, what would be your reaction?

19. What do you believe about hell? About heaven?

20. How confident are you right now of your salvation?

21. What do you believe is God's standard regarding sexual relationships within marriage? Sexual relationships outside of marriage?

22. When making a major decision, how do you determine God's will?

23. How strong are (were) your parents' spiritual convictions?

24. How much money (or percent of our income) should we contribute to the place where we worship?

25. What type of worship service do you prefer?

26. Is there a specific church or denomination that is important to you? Why?

27. Is there a particular church or denomination you would not want to be involved with? Why?

28. Was your divorce based on biblical grounds? How do you think God views your divorce? How have you reconciled your divorce with God and with yourself?

29. Are you willing to have a minister evaluate our current relationship? My previous relationship?

30. How would you adapt to attending a church where my former spouse attended?

31. Remarriage is viewed by many Christians as adultery. How do you deal with that stigma? Considered carefully, do you believe our marriage might be adultery? Why? Why not? How will we deal with people who believe it is?

# PART THREE

# Taking Action

*The first thing you ask yourself is: "Is this an important issue to me? To us?"*
*If your difference of opinion is on something that both of you consider insignificant, then you don't need to read any further. Simply go to the next question and enjoy discovering more about each other.*

Chapter 11

## How to Turn a Red Light to Green

If a particular red light is an issue that has significance for either of you, there is more than one conflict- resolution skill or approach available. We will not try to list them all for you. Our objective here is simply to give you a few ideas on how to approach the conflict. These approaches may or may not work for every yellow or red issue, but you should be able to make headway toward a green.

If these ideas do not work, we suggest that the two of you seek a qualified minister or counselor. Let that person see what you have discussed so far about the issue. Don't ever be concerned or embarrassed in seeking professional help. Your marriage is a precious asset and should be nurtured and cared for with wisdom. That usually takes more wisdom than any two people alone can provide.

Unfortunately, many times, one person or the other won't consider talking to a minister or counselor until one announces he or she is abandoning the relationship. Then the reluctant one is willing to talk, but in many cases it is too little, too late.

## Ideas to Consider

1. Express your thoughts and feelings openly yet sensitively. You cannot resolve a difference if you choose to be passive or silent.

2. Commit to the resolution of the disagreement and work on it. You cannot resolve a difference if one partner chooses to be less than 100 percent involved in making it work.

3. Realize the importance of the resolution of serious conflict. You can certainly live together without your red lights resolved, but your relationship will be weakened and possibly vulnerable to an affair or eventual divorce.

Once again, let us state clearly that we are here to help you make a wise decision. We want what is the very best for both of you. We are not for or against your getting remarried, assuming you are a widow or widower or have biblical grounds for your divorce. We are for your marriage if it will last the rest of your life. And we are against your marriage if it will eventually end in the pain of divorce.

It is our prayer that these questions helped you see with crystal clarity if your potential mate is to be your lifelong friend and spouse. We feel honored that you let us be a part of your decision-making process.

Chapter 12

---

*Ten Ways to Keep Your Marriage
Healthy and Happy*

The following ten suggestions will help keep you focused on developing a healthy, happy marriage.

1. Commit "till death do us part"—you have made a vow to God and to another much-loved human being.

   ✧ Dream together—look forward to things.

   ✧ Be loyal to your mate at all costs.

   ✧ Care more about what your mate thinks of you than what your friends do.

2. Develop a common spiritual commitment.

   ✧ Pray for your mate regularly.

   ✧ Pray together regularly.

   ✧ Worship together.

3. Want what is best for your lifemate.

   ✧ Focus on what's right with your mate, not what's wrong with him/her.

   ✧ Work as a team—rely on each other's strength.

   ✧ Serve your mate.

4. Spend time with model couples who have been happily married ten to twenty years longer than you.

✧ Develop a relationship with a personal mentor to help you when times are tough, someone to give you wise counsel.

✧ Spend time with peer couples that have healthy, happy marriages.

5. Understand that no marriage is perfect and no partner is perfect. Give grace to be different.

✧ No one wants to fail. Your mate is doing the best he/she can at the moment.

✧ Don't take all emotional explosions personally. Sometimes your mate just needs to let off steam!

✧ Let the relationship breathe. A couple needs time together and away. When things get tense, you may just need a few hours or days away.

6. Find time to communicate—walking on the beach, telephoning, traveling together.

✧ Communicating your heart
—Listen to your mate's heart, not just to words.
—Let your mate vent emotions without feeling you have to "fix it"!

✧ Settling differences
—Don't pout; stay and talk it out.
—"Clarify" your concerns if you don't like to "confront."
—Listen carefully. Allow the other to complete his/her thoughts without you interrupting, moving off the subject, or waiting impatiently to make your point.

7. Develop common interests.

  ⟡ Enjoy hobbies and friends.

  ⟡ Do fun things together—concerts, plays, picnics.

  ⟡ Travel together whenever you get a chance.

8. Get to know your mate at the deepest level possible.

  ⟡ Study your mate—what turns her/him off and on sexually, nonverbal signals, foreplay, moods, etc.

  ⟡ Know precisely what your mate needs from you.

9. Avoid:

  ⟡ negative kidding—saying negative things you don't really mean that secretly hurt and do serious damage to one's confidence and one's natural love;

  ⟡ conditional love—basing love on actions of any kind;

  ⟡ waiting for your mate to meet your needs before you will meet hers/his;

  ⟡ talking negatively about your mate's parents.

10. Be romantic, not just sexy.

  ⟡ Splurge occasionally.

  ⟡ Do small things which communicate "Thinking only of you . . . Thought of you while I was away . . . You are the center of my universe!"

  ⟡ Talk with a loving, caring, tender tone in your voice, not an angry, harsh, bitter tone.

## Ten Affordable Ways to Rekindle Your Romance

1. Take a little time off work—walk on the beach or in a forest, prepare a picnic away from everyone and everything, alone together.

2. Say "I love you" ten ways in one day without words.

3. Share something from your heart with your mate you have never told anyone about yourself.

4. Express every positive thought/feeling you have: "You smell good, I like your hairstyle, you have great hands, your voice is like the wind" (whatever you do, do not add "like a tornado"!).

5. Make your bedroom a special romantic place: use candles, lights, lace, etc.

6. Attend weddings and funerals together. It reminds you how fortunate you are to be alive and in love!

7. Give a few flowers, a bit of poetry, or a simple "just thinking of you" gift.

8. Call in the middle of the day just to say "I love you!"

9. A simple greeting card for no reason is very romantic—especially if it contains a short, loving, handwritten expression of the true love in your heart.

10. A full body massage is always nice—and is always affordable.

We hope these ten suggestions are as helpful to you as they have been to us.

# Conclusion

This book is intended to maximize your new marriage, not undermine it. Although some of the questions may seem threatening, look at them as an opportunity to learn more about yourself as well as your partner. As you both have a better understanding of each other, you will be able to handle the stresses that inevitably come in any marriage.

Choosing your life partner is, we believe, one of the most critical decisions you will make. You want to make the right decision, so you need to take the time and make the effort to be as certain as you can.

Remember: It's far easier to call off an engagement than it is to go through a divorce.

Disagreements on basic issues—unresolved red lights—need not be engagement breakers. You may just need help sorting out assumptions, understanding motivations, and clearing up communication. Don't hesitate to seek the help of a counselor to work through these differences. After all, a lifetime commitment is at stake.

These questions are not for one-time use. You can go through most of them once a year for the rest of your life and have fresh answers and gain new insights each time.

God wants family relationships to be secure, lasting, and mutually beneficial. It's our prayer that these questions have helped you make a wise and lifelong decision!

*Additional Resources
by Bobb and Cheryl Biehl*

**Asking to Win!**

This booklet (part of our Pocket Confidence series) goes in your suit coat pocket, briefcase, or purse. It contains one hundred questions—ten questions to ask in each of the following situations:

1. Asking—personal questions to avoid "small talk"

2. Brainstorming—to maximize your very finest ideas

3. Career-ing—when you or a friend are considering changing careers

4. Deciding—when a risky, pressurized, costly decision needs to be made

5. Interviewing—getting behind the smile of a potential team member

6. Focusing—putting your life into focus, or refocus

7. Organizing—to maximize your time

8. Parenting—to raise healthy, balanced children

9. Planning—any organization or major project

10. Solving—questions to solve problems faster

These booklets are packaged/priced reasonably enough for you to give to adult children, colleagues, friends, proteges, spouses, staff members.

## Career Change Questions / Lifework

*Thirty Questions to Ask before Making Any Major Career Change*

This series of thirty questions comes in handy any time you are thinking about the possibility of making a career change. These questions save you hours of uncertainty.

## Time-Focusing Questions

If it seems you just never have time as a couple to do what you most want to do, consider listening to this tape together and making some specific prioritizing decisions.

## Executive Evaluation-135

Have you ever wanted a comprehensive evaluation checklist for telling your mate exactly how he or she is doing, on a 1–10 scale, in everything from bad breath to decision making?

This is it—135 dimensions in all. This is an ideal annual tool for you to use with those close to you. And, if you like, let them evaluate you. This list helps maximize communication while concentrating on the positive.

## Focusing Your Life

*Focusing Your Life* is a simple, step-by-step process you learn in about three hours. It helps "clear the fog" and keeps you focused for the rest of your life. This great, personal retreat guide helps you reflect on your future!

## Mentoring: How to Find One and How to Become One

This booklet gives you very useful steps about forming a mentoring relationship and answers practical mentoring questions with tried and true answers. Consider finding a mentor couple to help you through some of the tight places in life.

## Mentoring Wisdom

As a couple you can grow together in your ability to provide wise leadership for your family and work settings. These principles are fun to read and discuss on a long vacation drive or when conversation gets a little stale and you need a small spark to get your discussion started.

There are approximately two hundred *quotable* leadership principles, rules of thumb, and observations which are key to generating creative ideas and gaining objective perspective!

## On My Own Handbook

If you have been increasingly concerned about your high school or college student's readiness to face the "real world," this book was written for your son or daughter.

Many adults have said that they wish their parents had taught them these principles before they started off "on their own." Parents, as well as students, benefit from these extremely fundamental leadership principles.

These principles will stay with your son or daughter for a lifetime. And they likely will pass many on to their children's children.

## Heart to Heart Series

We want you to have a perfect marriage, or as close to it as possible. These four affordable paperback books help you ask fresh, stimulating, fun, intimate, enlightening questions of your mate, to make sure your marriage has as solid a foundation as possible.

*Premarriage Questions*—Fun questions to ask before you get married, to help you have a healthy, happy, lifelong marriage.

*Newly Married Questions*—Intimate questions to ask each other on your honeymoon, to make sure you are bonded emotionally as well as physically as you start your life together.

*Anniversary Questions*—Stimulating questions to ask yourself on any anniversary, marriage retreat, or getaway weekend, to make sure your lines of communication are wide open!

*Pre-remarriage Questions*—Questions to ask before you remarry, to protect you both at this vulnerable time.

## Stop Setting Goals

When a husband is a goal setter and the wife a problem solver, there are many predictable problems. When a wife is a goal setter and the husband is a problem solver, there are many predictable problems. When both husband and wife are goal setters or both problem solvers, there are many predictable problems. This book helps you determine which you are, and how (as a couple) to maximize your differences instead of being hurt by them.

## The Question Book

A high percentage of marital frustration, tension, and pressure comes in the decision-making process. When unwise decisions are made without asking the basic, probing questions, it adds to the household tension.

Ninety-nine experts give you the twenty questions they would teach their own son or daughter to ask before making an important decision in their area of expertise.

*The Question Book* is a lifelong reference book. Written in a classic style, it will never really be "out of date." Topics are alphabetically easy to find.

### Where to Focus When Your Life's a Blur

Do you find yourself juggling the many hats of household taxi, travel agent, correspondent, nurse, tutor, coach, encyclopedia, psychologist, nutritionist, referee, and answering machine?

If this sounds familiar, this book gives practical, step-by-step help in sorting out your priorities and making choices that are best for you.

### Why You Do What You Do

This book is a result of more than 21,000 hours of behind-the-lines experiences with some of the finest, emotionally healthy leaders of our generation. This model was developed to maximize "healthy" people with a few emotional "mysteries" still unanswered! It answers questions (about your spouse) like:

✧ Why does he/she have a phobic fear of failure, rejection, or insignificance?

✧ Why is he/she so "driven" to be admired, recognized, appreciated, secure, respected, or accepted?

✧ Why is he/she an enabler, leader, promoter, rescuer, controller, people-pleaser?

✧ Why is he/she a perfectionist, workaholic, or "withdrawer" from tough situations?

✧ Where is he/she most vulnerable to the temptation of an affair?

✧ Why does he/she have such a hard time relating to his/her parents?

✧ Why does he/she sometimes seem like a child?

These and other emotional mysteries can be understood and resolved in the silence of your own heart and marriage without years of therapy.

**Wisdom for Men**

This is a small, easy-to-read gift book for any Christian husband. It contains life principles combined with parallel Scriptures to give wise perspective on many topics.

To learn when Bobb or Cheryl will be speaking in your area, or to learn more about any of the resources listed above, contact is possible in the following ways:

WRITE:

Bobb and Cheryl Biehl
c/o Masterplanning Group International
Post Office Box 952499
Lake Mary, Florida 32795-2499

TELEPHONE:

To contact the Biehl's office (answered "Masterplanning Group"), call 1-407-330-2028.

To request a complete catalogue (FREE), call 1-800-969-1976.

To order materials, call 1-800-443-1976

FAX: 1-407-330-4134